MW00456123

*J*BELIEVE
Jesus Loves
You

VALERIE PIERCE ANDREWS

ISBN 978-1-0980-0232-9 (paperback)
ISBN 978-1-0980-0233-6 (digital)

Copyright © 2019 by Valerie Pierce Andrews

All rights reserved. No part of this publication may be reproduced, distributed, or transmitted in any form or by any means, including photocopying, recording, or other electronic or mechanical methods without the prior written permission of the publisher. For permission requests, solicit the publisher via the address below.

Christian Faith Publishing, Inc.
832 Park Avenue
Meadville, PA 16335
www.christianfaithpublishing.com

Printed in the United States of America

To the glory of JESUS
My son—Brian Keith Andrews
My son—Barry Wayne Andrews
My grandson—Jake Henry Andrews
My granddaughter—Alanna Grace Andrews
Brian's wife—Laura Kilby Andrews
Barry's wife—Amanda Tolomei Andrews

Love one another, as I have loved you.

—John 15:12 (KJV)

Contents

Introduction

Believe Jesus loves you. These poems are telling a story. A story About what Jesus is. Jesus is love; he loves with a love that is above this earthly love.

The cover of this book has meaning:

(1) The color green represents life
(2) The dove represents the Holy Spirit
(3) The waterfalls represent a drink you will never thirst again. John 4:14 tells of this water.

John 3:16 tells of the love of Jesus. If you don't know Jesus, my prayer is you will find him.

Jesus loved you so much he died for you. Read Romans 10:8:13; this is a sinners prayer for salvation.

Mother
Dedicated to my Mother—Florence Pierce White

You're a sweet and beautiful lady.
You have lived through many trying days.
Yet you have grown more Christlike in many ways.
Joy, I pray, will greet thee today: maybe.
I am proud to call you "my mom."
You have inside beauty that glows through to your delightful smile.
Continues to travel to those lovely brown sparkling eyes for a while.
Two special words you practice each day: "Be calm."
Your simple Christian life is in need more every day.
The name of *Jesus* for many is never thought, neither do they say.
> May the Lord continue to bless: my dear mother and by the hand: *Jesus* will lead.

February 26, 1981

To My Mother
Dedicated to my Mother—Florence Pierce White

Just because you're you.
That's why I love you.
You were there when I needed you most.
When times were hard you pushed on and said, "I can. I must."
Times of struggle and heartache you saw and knew.
That extra encouragement you gave to see me through.
Love you for many more reasons and all these.
The godly life you live others sees.
A smile from you is a treasure of gold.
You are truly a mother mold.
Love you. Happy mother's day today and every day.
Read this little note each time you feel alone or blue, okay?

May 12, 1991

Brian

(To my son, Brian Keith Andrews)
This poem is in my book, *Fifty-Three Possible Moments*

You have always been very special to me.
A handsome young man with brownish blonde hair and
Two pretty blues to see.
With a note of wisdom sparkling from each eye,
Wisdom only comes from God, the Lord is eager for you
To try.
You are a true leader, that doth say,
"I believe in fair play."
Your academic ability is very high,
So reach beyond the stars and sky.
From a babe the Lord's hand has been on you.
The Lord has given talents of piano, writing, and
The trumpet too.
The Lord gave me a precious gift.
The Lord is waiting to give you a lift.
To love and serve him with all your heart.
The Lord gave me the honored mother's part.

October 2, 1980

Barry

(To my son, Barry Wayne Andrews)
This poem is in my book, *Fifty-Three Possible Moments*

A lad that is very special to me.
Very handsome, with a personality others would like the key.
Your academic ability much more than the average one.
Reach beyond the sky, your dreams, and the sun.
Talents, the Lord has given you.
Piano, writing, singing, and many more you will find too.
Swing from a limb, catch a frog, a worm, or just throwing a ball.
You appreciate the wonder of God and his handiwork of all.
You enjoy outside activities just as well in snow: A sleigh, a hill, and
    down you go.
With a smile that will melt any heart and bring laughter to a grim face.
You're a ray of sunshine in any place.
You're a joy that only God can bring.
Joy my heart doth sing.
The Lord is reaching for your hand.
Put your hand in his, and
Follow the footsteps of *Jesus* today.
Love and serve him all the way.

January 10, 1981

Jake
(To my grandson Jake Henry Andrews)

You are a very special and handsome young lad.
Your heart is good this gives others a smile of glad.
You were given a strong name for a reason you see.
You will always have a special place in the hearts of others and me.
A very likeable person treating all the same.
You can swim like a fish and play basketball like it was more than
A game.
Your kindness and love will give others a lift.
You were sent from God as a special gift.
You stand out in a crowd because of your respect for all.
Kindness will always keep you standing loveable and tall.
Your academic ability is very high,
So reach for the sky.
In your life I only play a small honored part.
Always let *Jesus* guide and love him with all your heart.

September 20, 2017
This was written on Jake's twelfth birthday (September 20, 2017)

Alanna Grace

(To my granddaughter: Alanna Grace Andrews)

You are sweet and adorable; all would say.
Your beauty is above the average girls of today.
You have double grace in your lovely name.
You have great favor in life to gain.
Amazing is your academic ability; now reading and writing the
Age of seven.
Can't imagine how beautiful and knowledgeable you'll be; when you
Reach the age of eleven.
Your interest and knowledge of dinosaurs shows a lot.
The ability to accomplishing anything in life, you truly have got.
You are a blessing from above.
Let your guiding light be love.
You have a special place in my heart.
Always let *Jesus* be your guide and never depart.

June 25, 2018

Laura
(To Laura Kilby Andrews)

You are a pretty young lady that believes in living right.
A wonderful personality with a loving spirit causes others to have
A morning happy and bright.
You are family-oriented; gifts and love you give.
You love to visit different places and see how the world lives.
You have many friends, love birthday parties, and work at a bank too.
Appreciate the fact you are a good wife and mother, and I love you.
Serve *Jesus*, let him guide each day, And love him all the way.

September 22, 2018

Amanda
(To Amanda Tolomei Andrews)

Amanda, you are lovely lady with black hair and sparkling brown eyes.
You master the health zone which is very wise.
You visit the market for organic foods that's in the healthy zone.
A good walk or work out for the bones.
You love the outdoors: hiking in the mountains and watching plants
  grow.
You love to cook for your family; this is another way for your love
  to show.
You have many gifts the Lord has given to you.
You can sing like a bird and love music too.
You are truly a blessing for all that can see.
You are a blessing to me.
In everything you say and do let *Jesus* be a part.
Love *Jesus* with all your heart.

September 25, 2018

Rosanna

To my sister: Rosanna Pierce Bishop

You were definitely given the correct name.
A beautiful flower with an abundance of grace.
Jesus was depicted as a rose and grace came on a cross at Calvary's place.
Scientist says a bumblebee is too heavy to fly.
You are like *Jesus*, you say things can be done, there's no how or why?
You want things done right a perfectionist to the tee.
When others stumble and fall you keep on going like a giant
    bumblebee.
This ability to sell furniture and other things too;
A job that requires skill and wisdom comes from above; you already knew.
Wisdom is a gift that you practice left and right.
You're sensitive to the Spirit; you reach out to others like a candle
Burning bright.
You have a smile to a room it gives light.
A loving personality that leads others on a road that is right.
Joseph in the Bible was favored of the Lord and some of his kin
Were jealous and hated him in his day.
But remember just like Joseph's deliverance: a winner and favor come
Your way.
Much ability and talents has been given you.
Jesus has chosen and anointed you too.
Rosanna a flower of grace now grows and lives;
You have so much to give.
The Lord has predestinated a work for you to do:
Only you can fill these shoes too.

April 17, 2002

SPIRITUAL
MOMENTS

Long Ago Love Died
To my friend—Carolyn Ferguson Adams

This large group of people are unusually loud;
They're crying, "Crucify him."
His innocence is unimportant to them.
Hatred is written on the face and shouts of this crowd.
Two thieves are condemned to die beside *Jesus* on a cross.
They have placed upon his head a wreath of thorns,
Piercing the flesh of his skin.
Oh, the back has many lashes from a whip they used then.
His blood is trickling freely from his head and back; cruel words and
Spitting they did toss.
The pain in his eyes, the sin of the world rested on him.
This huge cross has dropped from his hand;
His cross is lifted by a kind man.
Blood mingled with tears, where hate should have been for them.
They nailed him to a cross on Golgotha's hill.
Love filled his eyes and he cried, "Forgive them. They know not
What they do."
Love had died for my sins too.
Jesus arose the third day and he is forgiving sinners still.
Thank you, *Jesus* for your saving grace and dying in my place for me.
Jesus, you came to earth so long ago.
Yet you live within my heart, so
Your precious face I soon shall see.

Jesus died so we can go free.
The love of *Jesus* grew that day;
Grace and more grace came that day.

February 28, 1981

The Way to Calvary

Oh sinner, do you know the way to Cal-va-ry?
The way is found so eas-i-ly.
You will not need a light or trail to see.
Jesus has paved the way for you and me.
Jesus paid the price for all to see.
Long ago *Jesus* carried my sins to Calvary; there he died just
For me.
The trees were weeping then; the birds no longer found
A song to sing.
They knew these people were crucifying the Lord and King.
Jesus loved you so much; he willingly went to Cal-va-ry.
He suffered such agony as he carried the cross down a dusty
Road that led to Calvary, where he was nailed to a tree.
Sinner, come to *Jesus* now, only as a child.
Ask him to Forgive all your sins.
Say, "*Jesus*, I believe you died and rose from the grave.
Jesus, cleanse me within."
Don't you want to live forever in a glorious land?
A heavenly place where words can never convey the beauty,
Where death and heartache can never touch a child of the King,
Jesus is waiting for your call, "*Jesus,* come give me a song to sing."

March 11, 1981

Jesus Has Called

Jesus has called—the 12 disciples for a last supper.
Jesus has called—to tell of his crucifixion.
Jesus has called—"I thirst."
Jesus has called—"Forgive them."
Jesus has called—"It is finished."
Jesus has called—the tomb is empty, Jesus lives.
Jesus has called—Victory, the battle is over.
Jesus has called—suffered and died in your place.
Jesus has called—"Come follow me."
Jesus has called—"Ye shall be baptized with the Holy Spirit."
Jesus has called—"Disciples spread the *Good News*."
Jesus has called—sinners to repentance.
Jesus has called—for a full and meaningful life.
Jesus has called—always on the line to listen.
Jesus has called—"Watch ye and pray."
Jesus has called—"I will never leave you."
Jesus has called—"I am here with you."

April 14, 1981

Lord, My Prayer

Lord, help me learn my purpose here on earth.
Lord. help me realize the measure of my days, began at birth.
Lord, help me see the good in others.
Lord, help me not to condemn or talk about my sisters and brothers.
Lord, may my heart be filled with only love and kindness your
Will in mind.
Lord, bridle my tongue with gentleness and most of all love: your
     kind.
Lord, when I astray,
Lord, help me find my way.
Back to the loving *Jesus* of all;
That I may accomplish your call.

May 16, 1981
(Psalms 39:1–5, KJV)

Jesus the Scorekeeper

Jesus as the scorekeeper;
Would you be the seeker?
To find your place;
Ranked according to his pace.
Jesus as the scorekeeper;
Would you be the seeker?
The knowledge you've acquired throughout the years:
Do you fear the Lord or worldly fears.
Jesus as the scorekeeper;
Would you be the seeker?
Would he find in your heart wisdom kept;
And understanding, the fear of the Lord is the first step.
Jesus as the scorekeeper;
Would you be the seeker?
How do you find the standards the Lord gives?
Would you say, "To serve and love, according to his will every
Day you live?"
Jesus as the scorekeeper;
Would you be the seeker?

May 31, 1981
"But seek ye first the kingdom of God, and his righteousness;
And all these things shall be added unto you" (Matthew 6:33, KJV).

Riches

Riches or the desire for more than you need;
You struggle up the ladder of success;
Even though your family life is a mess.
A struggle all your life entitled "greed."
Riches or the desire for more than you need;
Corrupts the mind and spreads to your offspring.
Happiness is one thing riches will never bring.
Jesus is the answer, peace of mind and a security creed.
Riches or the desire for more than you need;
This is an indication *Jesus* doesn't lead.
Jesus the example, lay treasures, go to heaven
Is the plead.
Jesus is the ladder of success, and where he leads.

June 7, 1981
(Luke 18:19–25, KJV)

Time Oh Time
(Earth time is unlike *Jesus* time)

Time. Time oh time can change so many things.
Time, don't let me see:
What you have in store for me.
It can be your worst enemy,
Or a path that leads to eternity.
Time can heal a broken heart.
Where death has left a hurting part.
Time, time oh time can change so many things.
Time, don't let me see,
What you have in store for me.
Love is the only thing that will last;
No matter how far you search the past.
Love took my *Jesus* down a dusty road 'tis true,
And crucified *Jesus* as "King of the Jews."
Time, oh time can change so many things.
Time, don't let me see,
What you have in store for me.
As long as I have *Jesus* to see me through
Even if joy under weighs the saddest blue.
Time can't erase *Jesus* in my heart,
Nor the peace and joy *Jesus* gives from the start.

June 25, 1981

My Heart Cries

Dear *Jesus*, my heart is broken and sad.
The lump in my throat and the tear from my eyes
Have left me with many cries.
Lord, may your presence be more than a mere tad.
Assurance of better things ahead,
Your sweet presence flooding my soul;
Your will for my life being my goal.
Jesus, "Things work out for the best," these words
I must have read.
This is hard so many times to see,
When sickness or tragedy has touched a loved one.
At this time, dear *Jesus*:
I need the great love of *Jesus* the Son.
Words of despair intercede only through my heart that cries to
Thee.

July 24, 1981
"Many are the afflictions and heart aches of the righteous; but *Jesus*
Delivers and sets you free from all of them" (Psalms 34:19, KJV).

Jesus Is Victory

Lord, you have brought me oh so far.
The trying times came my way.
You're my rock and guiding light for each day.
I know you're "My bright and morning star.
You continue to love and bless my soul.
Failed and wandered astray, yet your mercy and love greets me.
Forgive my sins each time my heart confesses to thee.
The peace and joy that floods my soul: "the sweet story of ole."
Jesus, the King of the Jews.
Died a cruel death,
Nailed to a cross in my place,
Love glowed from his face.
A picture of love and pain until the last breath.
Third day…victory, the battle over and done;
He arose and now living in me.
Believe, Jesus Loves You is the key.
Followed by a closer walk, who will surrender to a plea, "Come."

August 10, 1981

Speak the Name—Jesus
To my son—Brian Keith Andrews and
his wife Laura Kilby Andrews

Look up when you're down and blue.
Listen to these words for the clue.
Just speak the name of *Jesus* it's like magic in that precious name.
The grave snatched a loved one and this road of thorns pieces from both
Sides of the lane.
Call on the Lord when life has brought you grief and pain.
Just speak the name of *Jesus* it's like magic in that precious name.
Has a tongue put you down because you live the Christian way?
Has someone betrayed you today?
Just speak the name of *Jesus* it's like magic in that precious name.
A disease has left you sick and frail.
Jesus. The healer and great physician as well.
Just speak the name of *Jesus* it's like magic in that precious name.
Jesus has saved your soul, so
You need the Holy Spirit to fill you from your head to your toes.
Just speak the name of *Jesus* it's like magic in that precious name.
If you need a friend to tell your troubles too:
To worship with or say, "I love you."
Just speak the name of *Jesus* it's like magic in that precious name.
He's always there just waiting for you,
To love him and praise him too.
Just speak the name of *Jesus* it's like magic in that precious name.

August 10, 1981
There is so much power in the name of *Jesus*.
Just speak the precious
Name: angels are waiting to help if you need help.
The name of *Jesus* is above every name.
Read Philippians 2:9–11, KJV

God's Tears

God grieved in his heart in Noah's day.
The sin of mankind was in practice in every way.
God destroyed them, flooding the land.
Forty days and forty nights of rain was the command.
Noah and family survived on an ark of gopher wood.
God's love reached out and Noah stood.
God grieves today because of sin;
History repeating the wickedness of men.
Could it be rain is a symbol of God's tears?
God has grieved for mankind throughout the years.
God reaches out with his love, mercy, and grace.
Noah walked with God, let it be your pace.
God's love is so great.
Don't be like mankind in Noah's day and wait too late.
God's tears will soon be joyously dry.
Jesus shall return to gather those that walked with God and
Shall be changed in the twinkling of an eye.

September 7, 1981
Read Genesis 2:5–6; Genesis 6:5–8; 1 Corinthians 15:51–58

God's Word

God's word created the heavens and earth.
God has given his healing word to the person with a new birth.
God's word the Bible directs your daily pathway.
God' word is bread for the spirit each day.
God's word is life; *Jesus* has paid the price at Calvary.
God's word is made of many promises for those that will see.
God's word is healing, "*By his stripes we were healed.*"
God's word is love on each page of the Bible:
God's love is sealed.
God's word is spoken by those that believe in *Jesus* the Son.
Praising the Lord and telling others what *Jesus* has done.
God's word is exciting knowing my heavenly home is near.
God's word is speaking only to those that will hear.

October 13, 1981
In the book of Genesis, it tells of the creation of the heavens and earth.
By his stripes we were healed over two thousand years ago 'cause
Jesus died to set us free.

Thank You, Lord

Thank you, Lord, for the refreshing and beautifying flowers that
Blossom in the spring.
Thank you, Lord, for the music coming from the birds that sing.
Thank you, Lord, for the sprinkling rain given to all living things.
Thank you, Lord, for joy, peace, and only good gifts do you bring.
Thank you, Lord, for the trees standing tall and free.
Thank you, Lord, for all the beauty you created and the eyes given
    to see.
Thank you, Lord, for the blessings you freely give.
Thank you, Lord, for health and a reason to live.
Thank you, Lord, for the sweet Holy Spirit dwelling in me.
Thank you, Lord, for the cross and taking my sins to Calvary.
Thank you, Lord, for loving me,
Open my eyes to your merciful and sacrificial love, so
I can really see.

October 26, 1981

Step by Step

Step by step *Jesus* is working in the believer's life.
Step by step 1ˢᵗ step, you were born again a new creation of the Lord.
Step by step 2ⁿᵈ step, walking and talking in the word of the Lord.
Step by step 3ʳᵈ step. *Jesus* is Lord and the filling of the Holy Spirit
Has come to give you power and understanding.
Step by step you're moving closer to the Lord.
Step by step the plan *Jesus* has for your life is coming into view.
Step by step *Jesus* is leading you into the discipleship of the Lord.
Step by step is the way you grow in the likeness of the Lord.
Step by step *Jesus* is leading those who will follow.

November 22, 1981

Jesus Is the Source

Hearing the word of God, faith cometh to the believer;
Open up your heart and be a receiver.
Faith can be as small as a mustard seed.
Will move mountains if you let *Jesus* lead.
Pray the prayer of faith to meet a need.
Believing *Jesus* is the source that answers each plead.
Give in order to receive.
Love is the motive for giving, believe.
Jesus will meet the need, ask in *Jesus's* name.
The promises of God are always the same.
God made and bought you so you're twice his.
God is love and listens to your prayers, no matter how large or
Small a request it is.
Jesus doesn't know the word impossible.
Ask and it shall be given, all things are possible.

January 20, 1982
"For with God nothing shall be impossible" (Luke 1:37, KJV).

Jesus—Lord of All

Jesus can't be Lord until he's Lord of all.
Jesus will come into the heart of a believer.
Only if you are willing to be a receiver.
Salvation is the first stepping stone.
Worldly things and pleasures can interfere and cause you to roam.
The second step will be postponed until you get your feet back on
The solid rock that leads to *Jesus* the Son.
Keep your heart, eyes, and mind on *Jesus*, and soon the last
Stepping stone will come.
The outstretched arms of *Jesus* are waiting for the last step this makes
     him
Lord of all.

February 9, 1982

Ignorance and Unbelief

Are you bound and chained with religion?
Has ignorance paved a road?
And unbelief carried the load?
Ignorance and unbelief ignores spiritual gifts.
Jesus can bring you out and the chains will he lift.
Let the Bible be your guide.
Don't let ignorance take the religious ride.
Jesus did things on earth as an example to mankind.
Learn of his miracles, healings, preaching, and teaching; this
Will educate your mind.
Sickness, disease, and poverty will be left behind with religious
    tradition.

December 9, 1981
Matthew 22 KJV, "*Jesus* is speaking to the scribes and Pharisees,
'Woe unto you hypocrites!'"
1 Corinthians 12, KJV tells about the spiritual gifts

Redeemed
(Delivered from sin and its penalties)

I am redeemed by the blood of the Lamb, and
I know that I am.
Jesus paid the price and salvation is mine.
He was led to the slaughter and there laid his life on the line.
I am redeemed by the blood of the Lamb, and
I know that I am.
He took all my sins, he took all my sickness, and he took all my
Poverty to Calvary.
I'm walking in a newness of life, can't you see?
I am redeemed by the blood of the Lamb: and
I know that I am.
Jesus wrapped me up in his love and came to live in my heart.
Jesus is walking with me teaching me the spiritual part.
I am redeemed by the blood of the Lamb, and
I know that I am.

March 2, 1982
Titus 2:14, KJV
Redeemed (definition) to get or buy back/rescue/to deliver from sin
And its penalties.

Jesus Temple

Are you building a *Jesus* Temple?
The foundation is words of life.
You must receive *Jesus* into your heart.
A temple for *Jesus* you can start.
Each stone is carefully molded into the image of
Jesus the Son.
Many benefits will result from the stone; more and more like Christ
    you
Will become.
Stones of this world do abound; only a chosen obedient stone is
Acceptable in building a spiritual dwelling.
Jesus, the chief cornerstone keeps each stone alive and telling.
Daily learning the life of *Jesus* and putting into practice love
For mankind.
This will also renew the mind.
Continue building this temple with the words of life. *Jesus* said, "I've
    come
To give life and give more abundantly."

April 5, 1982

Easter (Spell)

E is for eternity with *Jesus* for those who will receive *Jesus*.

A is for agony; *Jesus* paid the price for our sins.

S is for stripes, by his stripes were we healed.

T is for truth, *Jesus* is the true word; truth from heaven to set you
free.

E is for empty tomb; *Jesus* arose from the grave and conquered death.

R is for rent, the moment *Jesus* died on the cross the veil of the temple

Was rent from the top to the bottom; *Jesus* immediately

Became our advocate to the Father.

April 6, 1982

Advocate (definition) one who pleads another's cause.

"My little children, these things write I unto you, that ye sin not.

And if any Man sin, we have an advocate with the Father,

Jesus Christ the Righteous" (1 John 2:1, KJV).

Power in the Name (Song)

Chorus: I believe there is power speaking the name—
Jesus
I believe there is healing as close as his name—
Jesus
I believe he's the one who died for me—
Jesus
I believe he came to set me free—
Jesus
Chorus
I believe he delivers from sin, sickness, and poverty—
Jesus
I believe he crucified these at Calvary—
Jesus
Chorus
I believe the Holy Ghost is the power to overcome and see you
Through—
Jesus
I believe this power is given to the chosen few—
Jesus Chorus
I believe his word is life to a heart that will see—
Jesus
Jesus is the power that delivers and sets you free—
Jesus Chorus

May 21, 1982

By Faith—The Battle Is Over (Song)

Throughout the ages mankind has been on a battlefield; a battle
With death, a battle with sin, a battle with death, a battle with
Sickness, and a battle with poverty.
Jesus came down and won the victory that day at Calvary. Chorus
Some people never understand or have never been taught
Jesus Delivers and sets you free.
Reach out and take his hand and you will see,
Darkness into light you will be.
Walking daily in his word and you will find the key.

Chorus

The battle is over, the war has been won.
Jesus, the Savior, has paid the price for everyone.
Walking in his blessing and striving to be a blessing;
This is the victory in seeking the King.

July 11, 1982

Standing on His Word
(to Elizabeth Ann Bean)

Though the world has lost all hope: nothing is impossible when you're
Standing on his word.
Confessing the words of life will keep you on the victory road each day.
For those who will receive and for those who will say.
Though the world has lost all hope, nothing is impossible when you're
Standing on his word.
Standing on the words of life keeps you on the sunny side.
Joy comes from within, will always abide.
Though the world has lost all hope, nothing is impossible when you're
Standing on his word.
Standing on his word and believing in your heart ye shall receive.
No matter how impossible or what your five senses believe.
Though the world has lost all hope: nothing is impossible when you're
Standing on his word.

August 13, 1982
"For with God nothing shall be impossible" (Luke 1:37, KJV).

Jesus Made a Way

Jesus came to bring his people back to walk as
Kings and Priests again upon the earth.
Mankind was cursed, but *Jesus* made a way to receive a new birth.
He came to deliver his people from sin and the penalties of sin.
Redeemed from the curse of the law, poverty, sickness, death, and broken
Fellowship with the heavenly kin.
To really know him is to love him and receive his word into your
Heart.
Speaking the word daily until a root has developed and growing has
A start.
The seeds of Abraham live by faith day by day.
Speaking his word and acting upon his word no matter what
the circumstance come what may.
Jesus came and paid it all.
Now it's up to you to come and receive his call.

January 19, 1983
"Christ has redeemed us from the curse of the law, being made
A curse for us; for it is written, cursed is everyone that hangeth on a
tree" (Galatians 3:13, KJV).
"And if ye be Christ's then are ye Abraham's seed, and heirs according
to the promise" (Galatians 3:29).
Read—Galatians 3; Galatians 4:4–5; Deuteronomy 28

A Man Named Jesus (Song)

Chorus Come walk with me and talk with me: and
I will tell you about a Man named *Jesus*.

Chorus

How he walked the shores of Galilee.
How he healed the lame and set the captives free.
What he did that day at Calvary.
He took all my sins, he took all my sickness, took all my poverty
To a cross for you and me.
Jesus is living in me.
The Holy Ghost is living in me.
His words are life; the word is *Jesus*: now that word is living in me.
Giving power to speak the words of life setting me free.

Chorus

Listen and learn my friend to this story you see.
For *Jesus* is eager to dwell in thee.

September 16, 1982

Coming into Jesus (Song)

Chorus You've been in the valley; you've been on the mountain.
Now your searching for higher ground leads you into *Jesus*.
The wisdom of man has kept you bound.
The wisdom of God Will lead you into *Jesus*.
The Lord is now in the process of gathering his elect from the four
Corners of the earth.
If you look around, things are moving at a rapid pace not only in the
    natural
Realm but in a spiritual awaking: giving the mind a new birth.
You were predestinated from the foundation of the world and later
    sealed.
The Holy Ghost is the power to grow; the promise he willed.
Seek ye first the Kingdom of God and his righteousness and all the
Worldly things will soon shed at your feet.
This will lead you into *Jesus*, a heavenly meet.
The whole armor of God shall be put on by the chosen few.
This can only be done by subjecting yourself to his will a total process
Of the spirit, soul, and body too.

November 12, 1982
(Matthew 6:33, KJV)

Darkness into Light (Song or Poem)

Chorus He's bringing his people out; he's bringing his people out.
He's bringing his people out; out of darkness into light.
You've been in the wilderness oh much too long.
Searching and reaching but never knowing where you
Were bound.
Jesus is that light and worldly things has kept darkness all
Around.
You may be rich, you may be poor, you may have never step
Foot in a church door.

Chorus

You've been on a worldly battlefield, now
Jesus is coming in
View.
You are one of the chosen few.
The time set especially for your pace.
You are a son of God born into a heavenly race.

Chorus

Receiving the word line up line, precept upon precept; the
Jesus way is growing.
The whole armor of God will surely be your clothing.

March 28, 1983
(Isaiah 28:9–10, KJV)

Changing (Song or Poem)

Chorus Changing…changing…
God's people are changing: putting the
Old life down because you're changing…changing.
Jesus is the word and now that word is growing in me.
Believing his word over the fleshly realm is step by step you see.

Chorus

You have so much to gain today.
Reaching for the *Jesus* life is the only way.

Chorus

Walking in newness of life, singing a new song.
Your past is getting dimmer and it won't be long.

Chorus

The sons of God are reaching, now in view.
The whole armor of God is for the chosen few.

Chorus

May 30, 1983

Come to the Water
(Song or Poem)

Jesus said, "Come to the water." *Jesus* said,
"I'll give you life forever."
A river of life springing up, a living word that can never die.
Jesus is that river and this is his cry.
Drink from this water; athirst you never will be.
Because in *Jesus* the truth will set you free.
Refuge from the storms of life, sheltered and protected in *Jesus* name.
You'll be so blessed you'll never be the same.
This living word renews the mind each day.
Changing your ways to the *Jesus* way.

August 29, 1983

Jesus Is Everything (Song or Poem)

When you say *Jesus* you've said everything.
When you say *Jesus* you've
Said it all; *Jesus* is everything to me.
He's my bread when I'm hungry.
He's my water when I thirst.
He's the rock I stand upon when life's storms have come my way.
He's my bread when I'm hungry.
He's my bread when I thirst.
He's the water that's living.
He's the bread the words of life.
He's the King of all Kings
He's the Lord of all Lords.
He's the one that set me free at Calvary.
He's the one that died for me.
He lifted me up with his love and grace.
He believed in me,
The day he took my place.
Now everything can be found and *Jesus* is the key.
Jesus is the word that sets the captives free.

October 25, 1983

Tell Me That Story
(Song or Poem)

Oh tell me that story—again, how
Jesus can free you from sin.
Sin will vanish away;
Oh this very day.
Oh tell me that story—again, how by his stripes
I'm healed.
Sickness will vanish away:
Oh this very day.
Oh tell me that story—again, how
Jesus became poor that we might
Be rich.
Poverty will vanish away;
Oh this very day.
Oh tell me that story—again, how
Jesus conquered death.
Death will vanish away;
Oh this very day.
Oh tell me that story—again, how
Jesus died on the cross; he freed me
From sin, he freed me from sickness,
he freed me from poverty. And
he freed Me from death.
Oh tell me that story—again.

My friend won't you see,
How *Jesus* can set you free.
Oh tell me that story—again.

October 25, 1983

Praise You, Jesus
(Song or Poem)

Chorus

They crucified the Lord.
They crucified the King.
They nailed him to a tree.
He sacrificed himself at Calvary.
He shed his blood and now it covers me.
Oh praise you, *Jesus*, what you did that day.
You made a way where there was no way.
You saved me from a world of sin.
You gave me life where death had been.

Chorus

Oh praise you, *Jesus*, what you did that day.
Your love believed in me and caused a way.
By his stripes healing belongs to me.
You unlocked the door to paradise and your great love was the key.

Chorus

December 13, 1983
Paradise—(definition) The Garden of Eden, Heaven, happiness. Any
place or state of perfection, etc.

Success

My destiny I saw in a dream.
Success is a seed that came from within.
My goal today, "Do my best and then."
Dreams and reality meet and success materializes from the
World of the unseen.

January 20, 1983

Jesus Is the Way

Your goal is set, your vision high and Jesus is the way.
This trial you're going through; you must remember this, you're one
Step closer than you were yesterday.
Speaking the words of life, it's all up to you.
The flesh is a battle and at times it's been hard, but *Jesus* will come
Shining through.
Honor and praise goes to *Jesus* because his great love
Paved the way.
The sacrifice he made at Calvary unlocked the chains of even death
That day.
With death defeated life in *Jesus* is found.
Confessing the word will keep you *Jesus* bound.

March 6, 1984

God's Flowers

Prettiest little flowers a blooming in the spring.
The brightest colors: I have ever seen.
They wake the morning declaring their beauty from
God's coloring book.
No one but the Master *Jesus* could create this look.
Jesus died in your place that you might be a flower.
His word is the spring shower.
The world and your carnal mind is where your growth in
The Lord is spurred.
A budding flower is abiding in life growing daily by the watering
Of the word.

March 16, 1984

Jesus Is at the End of the Road (Song or Poem)

Chorus

Jesus is at the end of the road.
The way may be narrow and heavy be the load.
Trials may come and tears may fall.
To know him just as he is will be worth it all.
The outstretched hands of *Jesus* is at the end of the road.
Many sharp stones and curves the devil has sowed.
Keep your eyes on *Jesus* and he will see you through.
Jesus sought you and bought you and now it's all up to you.

Chorus

The sons of God are rising with the message of truth.
"New and Living Way."
Jesus is the way; he conquered death and sickness and brought back
A new day.
His love paved the way where there was no way.
Jesus is waiting for a renewing of the mind; the word of God be
    rooted
Enough to say.

Chorus

May 9, 1984

To See Jesus

Open our eyes Lord We want to see *Jesus*
Open our eyes Lord We need to see *Jesus*
Open our ears Lord We want to hear *Jesus*
Open our ears Lord We need to hear *Jesus*
Open our mouths Lord We want to teach *Jesus*
Open our mouths Lord We need to teach *Jesus*
Open our minds Lord We want to know *Jesus*
Open our minds Lord We need to know *Jesus*
Open our hearts Lord We want to praise *Jesus*
Open our hearts Lord We need to praise *Jesus*
Born of his spirit Washed in his blood
Mold and make us
In the likeness of *Jesus* Open our eyes Lord

June 20, 1984

The Mystery of Jesus (Song or Poem)

People are solving mysteries every day.
Looking in every direction to find the way.
But the greatest mystery this world could ever know is found
In the name of *Jesus*.
Chorus His name is *Jesus*
His name is *Jesus*
The King of all Kings
The Lord of all Lords
His name is *Jesus*
There is no secret in knowing what God can do.
But the mystery is found at Calvary: only the blood of *Jesus*
Could cover you.
That power is over sickness, death, and it's found in the name
Of *Jesus*.

Chorus

October 30, 1984

A New Song

We're walking in a new day.
Singing a new song that's never
Been sung before.
Jesus unlocked the door.
The chains of death and sickness are there no more.
It's all up to you to open the door.
Jesus paid the price.
Jesus now has the keys to death and life.
We're walking in a new day singing a new song that's never
Been sung before.
Walking in blessings where lack and want cease to be no more.
Jesus said love me and walk in my ways.
I will reveal myself unto you in that day.
Jesus unlocked the chains where sin and unbelief did have
The keys.
The door to life is open for those with eyes to see.

March 22, 1985

How Big Is My God (Song or Poem)

He created this whole universe and knew me from the start.
Yet he lives within my heart.
How big is my God; there is no beginning.
How big is my God; there is no end.
He can calm the raging storms at sea.
Open the blinded eyes to see.
How big is my God; there is no beginning.
How big is my God; there is no end.
He came down from heaven to redeem mankind.
He died up there on Calvary, defeated the darkness of the mind.
How big is my God; there is no beginning.
How big is my God; there is no end.
Sin and death no longer reigns when *Jesus* sets you free.
The chains are broken, even now for those with eyes to see.
How big is my God; there is no beginning.
How big is my God; there is no end.

July 13, 1985

Jesus the Word

You brought me through a world of fear.
You kept me when no hope was near.
Knew me before the world was made.
In your mind the plans were laid.
Defeated death and crossed the line.
Brought me and now life is mine.
Your word restores and brings me back.
Renews my mind where there is no lack.
Your word is rooting out the seeds that Satan has sown.
Planting the seeds of life that's getting into my bones.

August 7, 1985

Safe and Secure

You don't have to worry, you don't have to weep.
I know a secret that no one can keep.
He made you a winner when he rose from the grave:
Defeated sin and death now, you can be saved.
Safe and secure from the world and its cares;
Jesus is the answer and his love you must share.

October 5, 1985

Think of Calvary

Sometimes I feel discouraged: sometimes I feel blue.
I think of Calvary and I know what I must do.
You came down from heaven to rescue me.
You became sin so I could go free.
Sometimes I feel discouraged; sometimes I feel blue.
I think of Calvary and I know what I must do.
You paid the price, bought me back that I could be a part of you.
Now I have a joy within that comes from knowing you.
You are the breath I breathe; you are the song I sing.
Praises to *Jesus*; I joyfully bring.
Sometimes I feel discouraged; sometimes I feel blue.
I think of Calvary and I know what I must do.
This fleshly part of me must bear its cross too.
How much I love you Lord, will be revealed in what I do.

October 6, 1985

Full of Life

We must be strong…unmovable…and full of life.
Pressing onward…to that heavenly light.
We must set our love on…
Jesus, then our eyes will have
Single sight.
We must be strong…unmovable…and full of life.
Keeping our mind…on the things from above;
We must be…ever learning the word…
God's love.

February 11, 1986

Rest in Jesus

Many times I have been tossed about;
But *Jesus* always brought me out.
He lifts you up and sets your feet on solid rock.
You will find a rest there in *Jesus*.
A place where only eagles fly.
A new song that only a few will try;
They have left their earthly cry;
And found wings that will never die.
Many times I have been tossed about,
But *Jesus* always brought me out.
He lifts you up and sets your feet on solid rock.
You will find a rest there in
Jesus; your eyes will detect things
In a different light.
Love beyond understanding when
Jesus gives you sight.
Peace and joy the world knows nothing.
A song in your heart the world can never sing.

February 10, 1986
Psalms 103:5; Isaiah 40:31

Making Me Whole

This word is making me whole.
Sifting out the darkness that's clouded my soul;
Jesus you came and gave me this light;
And from the world it's giving me flight.
This word is making me whole.
Sifting out the darkness that's clouded my soul:
Where fear and death had such a hold;
Through his redeeming blood;
I was made whole.
This word is making me whole.
Sifting out the darkness that's clouded my soul;
Finding my place, setting me free.
This word of God is storing me.

March 12, 1986

Jesus Paid It All

To Tammi Pierce Anderson

Turn back the pages of time and you'll see.
Jesus paid it all so you could go free.
He knew his destiny before the world was made.
Yet he created man and the plans were laid.
Turn back the pages of time and you'll see.
Jesus paid it all so you could go free.
In the garden man had fell and sin did abound.
The tree of life was no longer around.
Turn back the pages of time and you'll see.
Jesus paid it all so you could go free.
Jesus came down from heaven; they nailed him to a tree.
His redeeming blood says now you go free.
Turn back the pages of time and you'll see.
Jesus paid it all so you could go free.
God's amazing love (grace) reached down to man.
Jesus is the tree of life, so eat the word while you can.

March 24, 1986

John Saw a City

John saw a city coming down, down, down.
And it will not be long until they're all found.
It's not a city that's made by hands,
Or a city that's made by man.
But a holy city made by the word.
This word is *Jesus* and no man can undergird.
It's a river of life, flowing down, down, down,
And a light for the world all around.
It's the glory of the Lord shining through.
It's a people from the foundation he knew.

May 30, 1987
Undergird (definition) to support or secure by a rope or the like passed beneath.

He Knows Me

He knew me then and he knows me now.
He wrote my name in the Book of Life,
And he said now you have life eternally.
He knew me then and he knows me now.
He lifted me from this earthly cry,
And he said now I have set you on high.
He knew me then and he knows me now.
The blood of *Jesus* covered me,
And he said now my redeeming blood sets you free.
He knew me then and he knows me now.
Jesus said I've opened a door
To life and blessings forevermore.

June 1, 1987

Word of Life—Restoring

Too many sunsets have gone behind those mountains and too
Many rivers I've had to cross.
Too much darkness has clouded my mind, but *Jesus* gave me light.
From this world it has given me flight.
Too many sunsets have gone behind those mountains and too
Many rivers I've had to cross.
But now I'm on a journey that grows sweeter every day;
I'm finding my place, and *Jesus* is the way.
Too many sunsets have gone behind those mountains and too
Many rivers I've had to cross.
Time has taken a toll,
But this word of life is restoring back what the devil has stolen.

October 14, 1987

The Word—Across the Land

He's stretching forth his word across the land.
Reaching out his hand to fallen man.
There's a new song in the air; there's joy to be found.
He's stretching forth his word across the land.
Reaching out his hand to fallen man.
Jesus made a way in a land that was bound.
He's stretching forth his word across the land.
Reaching out his hand to fallen man.
Love found a way.
Power and victory has come today.

February 24, 1988

Victory Is Mine

He's alive he's alive; he has risen from the grave.
He's alive; death is defeated; victory is mine.
He's alive he's alive; the tomb is empty; victory is mine.
There's no grave that could hold him; Satan is defeated;
Victory, victory is mine.
Now he's risen in power and victory to set me free.
He's my savior and my Lord; he's the one that I adore.
Victory, victory, his love paid it all for me.
Victory, victory is mine.

April 6, 1988

Darkness Flees

When your eye is single on *Jesus*, darkness can't find the way.
Jesus has the answer come what may.
So keep your eyes on *Jesus* because he is the light.
He's the everlasting Father; he's everything right.
You'll walk in the kingdom and light of life can be yours.
To restore the body and cause blessings to come your way
Forevermore.

February 21, 1989
(Matthew 6:21–24)
(Genesis 3:5–7, KJV)

The Most Expensive

The most expensive thing;
What answer can you bring?
Diamonds, pearls, a mansion on a hill,
Pot of gold, or maybe a hospital bill.
There's no answer that can compare,
To the most expensive thing I wish to share.
Sin is the most expensive thing to visit this earth.
Jesus paid the price when death had given birth.
Death goes back to Adam and Eve our kin.
Jesus has freed us from the penalty of sin.
Death is defeated; victory over death is renewing the mind.
What *Jesus* did that day has been hidden from mankind.

March 21, 1989
Read Genesis

A Holy Nation (Song)
To my friends who love *Jesus*

We are God's people, a Holy Nation;
He knew from the foundation.
A Holy Nation
We are God's people washed in the blood of the Lamb;
Born of his Spirit: clothed in his righteousness.
We are God's people, a Holy Nation, a Holy Temple set
Upon a hill, a light for the people.
We are God's people, *Jesus* has suffered all.
Jesus has paid it all; *Jesus* has given all to his people.
Praises we give to him
Honor we give to him
We are God's people, a Holy Nation.
A Holy city, a river of life, love for all people.
We are God's people, a Holy Nation.

August 17, 1988

Victory Was Bought

Victory was bought at Calvary
Jesus knew it took redemption for you and me.
His love reached out beyond measure.
He looked into time, there you and me, his treasures.
Jesus laid down his life, now you go free.
I've redeemed you back, now you belong to me.
Death is defeated; victory was bought at Calvary.
He made a way so we could go free.
Victory was bought at Calvary.
Jesus knew it took redemption for you and me.
He laid down his life and now you go free.
I've redeemed you back, now you belong to me.

August 27, 1990
Redeem (definition) to get or buy back; recover to set free; Rescue, to deliver from sin and its penalties.

Cleaning Me Up

Thank you, Lord, for what you're doing in my life.
You're cleaning me up and taking out the part that's not like you.
I have struggled for so long; I know it's true.
Jesus. I want to be just like you.
Just like Joshua and Caleb by faith they went into the Promised Land.
Finding your precious promises by faith I'm reaching out and
Taking your hand.
Thank you, Lord, for what you're doing in my life.
You're cleaning me up and taking out the part that's not like you.
Sin and death had me bound.
The *Jesus* life I have found.
I'm growing in you, restoring my mind, setting me free.
Praise *Jesus* for what you did at Calvary.

September 13, 1990

What Is Thanksgiving?

Once a year the family will gather
To be thankful and see each other.
Talk about the weather. Cost of living,
eat too much turkey, dressing,
Vegetables, and pumpkin pie.
After eating too much, reach for the
Rolaids with a big sigh.
What is Thanksgiving?
Thanksgiving is giving thanks to *Jesus* every day.
Thanking him for the cross and keeping the cross before you to
Guide your way.

November 21, 1990

Faith, Power, and Victory (Song)

Miracle can happen…love found a way.
Jesus is the miracle…a miracle of life.
He gave his life…that we could live.
Faith, Power, and victory today.
When you've found love…you've found
Faith, power, and victory.
Miracles can happen…love found the way.
Faith, power. and victory will overcome the world.
Jesus is the miracle; love found the way.
Faith, power, and victory today.

July 8, 1991

Life Message

As I walk this troubled land,
I see the devil has the upper hand.
He's deceived the world in all the things that are true.
What about all the things *Jesus* has done for you?
Jesus knew from the beginning the devil had a plan.
Keeping the message of life hidden from man.
Read the end of the book and you will sing:
Praises and love to *Jesus* you'll bring.
There's coming a day,
When all of God's chosen people will have the say.
They'll speak the words of life to a dying world.

May 19, 1993

Joy, Joy, Joy
To my friend Wanda Kabutan

Joy, joy, joy in my soul,
And I know who made it so.
Came down to earth so long ago,
And paid a debt I did owe.
He's the joy of my soul
And I do love him so.
Joy, joy, joy in my soul,
And I know who made it so.
Words of life; who will receive;
A giver of life who will believe.
A joyful song I will raise;
Sing of his love and give him praise.
Joy, joy, joy in my soul,
And I know who made it so.
Jesus the sweetest song and sound I know;
His love has made it so.
Exceeding great and precious promises has found me always,
And I'll praise him all my days.

July 4, 1993
Read 11 Peter 1–4
Exceeding (definition) surpassing; extraordinary; extreme.
Exceed—to go or be beyond.

Jesus Is the Reason
To my friend Carolyn Ferguson Adams

You are the reason that I live today.
You are the reason that I sing this way.
You were there in the darkest of hours.
You were there even when there were no prayers.
You are the reason that I live today.
You are the reason that I sing this way.
I knew it was you, Lord, a prophet foretold.
You sent down your word to renew my soul.
You are the reason that I live today.
You are the reason that I sing this way.
Yes, I love, I love this man, this man of Galilee.
Jesus came to change and set me free.

January 9, 1994

The Truth Is Jesus
(Song or Poem)

Search for truth you'll find love; you'll find the Lord.
The truth you'll find in the love of *Jesus*.
The world and cares of this world has been your boss.
You'll find the truth at the foot of the cross.
The truth of *Jesus*, it's in his love for you and me.
Truth is in the blood that flows from Calvary.
Redeeming power pure and holy flows from Calvary.
Giving life, sacrificial love grew on the tree.
Jesus broke the reigning law of sin and death.
Life was stronger; *Jesus* is the breath.

August 27, 1994

Praise Jesus (Song or Poem)

Jesus, we've come into this place this night
To honor and praise your name it's right.
Jesus, we praise you, *Jesus,* we thank you, *Jesus,* we love you,
Jesus, we honor you this night.
Lift up holy hands and praise your holy name.
Our hearts are filled with thanks; our God who's always the same.
Songs of praise we will bring; Praises to the King of Kings.

July 20, 1995

The Real Light

This darkness of religion that has filtered and corrupted the mind;
The hidden truth: death is defeated and redemption is mine.
Jesus said you are no longer children of the night.
All darkness will be brought to light.
The simplicity of God's light all will not see.
Christ has risen; darkness defeated for you and me.
God said, "Let there be light" and called the light day.
More light, the more understanding of *Jesus* is coming your way.
Walk in light, the word shines bright.
Jesus is the truth the light.
Believing, loving, and praying is being real.
Be a willing vessel yielded and still;
Jesus knocks with the light of life on our hearts door.
Light is being real and light is *Jesus Christ* forevermore.

July 24, 1995
Genesis 1:3–5; John 1; 1 John 5:7; Matthew 5:14–16
Psalm 27:1; Psalm 119:105; Ephesians 5:8; Colossians 1:12–14
Real (definition) existing or happening as or in fact, actual. true. etc.
Authentic; genuine.

Press On
(To John Alan Bishop)

When death knocks at the door,
And Satan opens the door. Press On!
When loneliness and grief has tormented,
You don't understand and your mind becomes more tormented.
Press On!
Clouds of doubt, discouragement has clouded your mind.
Your total existence is put on the line.
Press On!
Persecution has come to torment today.
Promises of God outweigh anything that comes your way.
Press On!
Those that seek shall truly find.
For the Kingdom of God can truly be mine.
You must press into the kingdom realm.
Eyes on *Jesus*, the word from heaven; these are the keys given to
Those chosen by him.
Press On!

February 25, 1996
"I press toward the mark for the prize of the high calling of God in
Christ Jesus" (Philippians 3:14).

Be a Butterfly

Mankind is depicted as a worm after the fall of Adam and Eve in that
time.
There's a thin line be a butterfly or a worm you choose.
Jesus paid the price; you can win or lose.
God's word is the changing force in finding that fine line.
The butterfly soars above this religious system and this death realm.
Finding truth is finding flowers of happiness soaring in the sky.
The Kingdom of God forms the cocoon that gives wings to fly.
Flying high is daily truth: spreading your wings so you can be with
him.

April 16, 1996
"But they that wait upon the Lord shall renew their strength; they
shall mount
Up with wings as eagles: they shall run, and not be weary; and they
shall
Run, and not be weary; and they shall walk, and not faint" (Isaiah
40:31).

Another Mountain
(To my sister) Marilyn Bumgarner

Another hill to climb
Another mountain ahead *Jesus* will see you through.
Jesus will always be there for you.
Another hill to climb another mountain ahead
Need to move that mountain out of your way.
Jesus sent the word; faith unlocks the door today.
Another hill to climb another mountain ahead
Speak the word only; it shall be done.
Jesus paid the price and we've already won.
Another hill to climb another mountain ahead
Jesus sent the light from heaven above.
Covered by the blood; God's perfect Love.
Another hill to climb another mountain ahead
More than anything, seek his face,
Led by the Spirit; now take your place.
Another hill to climb another mountain ahead
By faith you will know;
Speak to the mountain; the mountain must go.

April 28, 1996

I'm Going Through
(To Kevin Shumate)

Thou I walk through this valley of tears;
Somehow time has turned into years.
I'm *Going through*
The past has a way of playing on the mind.
Discouragement, loneliness, and unworthiness you'll find.
I'm Going through
Storm clouds gather around me clawing at my mind.
I'm going through because I've crossed the line.
I'm Going through
When darkness comes dimming your way.
God's light of understanding will guide; come what may.
I'm Going through
Jesus will see you through;
He'll restore and be there for you.
I'm Going through
Jesus is the winning side.
Words of life is words of light to see you
Through.

August 27, 1996
"Restore unto me the joy of thy salvation; and uphold me with thy
Free spirit" (Psalms 51:12).
"For the joy of the Lord is your strength" (Nehemiah 8:10).

Jesus Is Truth
(To Steven Shumate)

Jesus came to seek and save.
Jesus came to heal and deliver.
Jesus came to be an example.
Jesus came to forgive sin.
Jesus came to bring understanding.
Jesus came to conquer death.
Jesus came to redeem back.
Jesus came to give life.
Jesus came to show the way.
Jesus came to be the way.
Jesus came to bring the truth.
Jesus came to a chosen few.
Now it's all up to you.
He's done all and paid the price too.
The way to life is the narrow way.
Only a few will seek the truth this day.
Seek the truth; you will find light.
Jesus is the truth and a light shining bright.

February 7, 1997
Jesus came to earth because he loved us so very much.
This whole world was created because he loved us so very much.
Please read: Romans 8:34–35; Psalms 119:105

Don't Look Back
(To Melissa Pierce)

The children of Israel saw miracles and miracles.
They saw the power of God and their deliverance was given to
      Moses's hand.
Whatever came out of their mouth was theirs, but they couldn't
Possess the land.
Looking back and complaining you will remain.
The Israelites proved you will soon die and never gain.
We have a promise like the children of Israel; what we speak out of the
Mouth we shall possess.
Angels are ministering Spirits; looking back and complaining is
A mess.
Provoking an Angel, destruction is at hand.
Learning to speak the Word you will possess the land.

November 10, 1998
Read Exodus 23:20–21; Psalms 103:20

The Christmas Light
(To my granddaughter: Alanna Grace Andrews)

There was a natural light,
The wise men followed that night.
This was a sign, the light, the understanding of God's word was near.
When *Jesus* died on the cross; it was finished; the revelation of
His word was here.
The light of life, deliverance, and understanding was no longer lost.
The first Christmas light hung on an old rugged cross.
Jesus said, "I am the light of the world come and follow me."
Jesus is the light, the only light for the dark world to see.
The light, a learning process is renewing the mind.
The light, will cause his people to shine.

December 16, 1998
Then spake Jesus again unto them, saying,
I am the light of the world:
He that followeth me shall not walk in darkness.
but shall have the light of life. (John 8:12)

When I Needed Love

When I needed love
I said hello, you made a reply;
That I just wanted to cry.
When I needed love
A word of encouragement to lighten my day;
Words to burden me came my way.
When I needed love
Be a friend and be there for me.
No time, and you didn't see.
When I needed love
Jesus died 2000 years ago;
Love was extended as you know.
When I needed love
Jesus arose from the tomb in three days.
Death was defeated in all its ways.
When I needed love
Jesus forgives and sets you free;
A love that's there for you and me.

March 26, 1999
Please read: Proverbs 10:12; Ephesians 3:19; John 3:16–17; 1 John
    4:7–21
(Jesus Is love)

Thank You, Jesus (Song)

Yes he proved his love one day:
Jesus died on that cruel tree.
He died to set me free.
And I thank *Jesus*…
Yes I thank him for the love
Yes I thank him for the love
That he has shown me.
When I think of what he has done;
All the love that he has shown;
And I know who holds the key to life and its mysteries.
And I thank *Jesus*
Yes I thank him for the love
Yes I thank him for the love
That he has shown me.
Thank you, Jesus
Thank you, Jesus
Thank you, Jesus

May 31, 1999

Christmas Is Joy, Peace, Grace, Life, And Love

To my grandson: Jake Henry Andrews

Jesus is that bundle of joy that came to give us joy.
Joy unspeakable and full of glory; *Jesus* came as a baby boy.
Angels came singing for unto you a child is given; peace on earth goodwill to all.
God's grace came the plans laid and the cross was his
Destiny call.
This bundle of life came to give life.
When *Jesus* arose from
The tomb, death no longer reigned.
Love came in a bundle that night.
Love reached with a Ruling force.
Love caused four others to be gained.
Joy Peace Grace Life
The greatest of these is love.
When love reigns Christmas in Your heart.
This great love; the message of life will grow as a seed:
Producing and never departs.

December 7, 1999
"And now abideth faith, hope, charity, these three; but the Greatest of these is charity" (1 Corinthians 13:13).
(Charity—the love of God)

Jesus Sets You Free (Song)

When I needed love who came and rescued me?
When I cried a tear, who caused a song in my heart?
(chorus) *Jesus, We Worship You*
Jesus, We Thank You
Jesus, We Love You
Jesus, We Praise You
When you looked at me, you saw only what I could be.
When darkness covered my mind, who came and brought the light?
Now I see.

(chorus)

When I needed life, who came and conquered death.
When I needed love, who came and rescued me? (chorus)

December 8, 1999
Love causes the heart to sing. and the light of *Jesus*
You can always find the right road; when *Jesus* leads
The way.

The Love of Jesus (Song)

Let the love of *Jesus* shine through,
And you'll see what *Jesus* will do.
He'll turn those dark clouds into day.
The love of *Jesus* will guide your way.

(Chorus)

Let the love of *Jesus* shine through,
And you'll see what *Jesus* will do.
He'll take a life and make it brand new.
The light of understanding he'll give to you.

(Chorus)

Life word coming from the heart of you;
He'll break the chains of death too.

(Chorus)

December 8, 1999

Spring—To Appear Suddenly
(Favorite time of the year, *spring*)

This time is but a season:
Stop enjoy, give you the reason.
Even the birds have changed their tune;
Singing for life to appear soon.
(Songs of life, new beginnings, a fresh ring)
Bees are buzzing even they have something
To say.
Letting you know honey is on the way.
The flowers are beautifying the grass of green.
Thank *God* for all you've seen.
(Freely given, what joy it truly brings.)

March 20, 2000
(March 20, 2000—today spring begins)

A Love Letter

To my son and his wife Barry Wayne Andrews
and Amanda Tolomei Andrews

A love letter written to the author of love;
You came with a message of love from above.
Your actions, words, every cell of your being crying out love to man;
Not to condemn but to deliver, learn to love you can.
The words "I love you" is in vain;
If action has not followed and remained.
Love doesn't push, control, or tries to have its way.
Love reaches out always giving every day.
Love is a light that burns bright;
Where darkness ruled it will take flight.
Love never stops it is continually growing;
Faith, hope, kindness, patience, forgiveness, always sowing.
The love walk is a driving force for all your needs to be met.
Healing, wounded heart, hurt feelings, grief, loneliness, healing
Of the bones, all this and more you get.
Walking in love you will live, think, speak, and act a new way.
You will become an overcomer and joy, peace, and
Righteousness is for today.
Love is like a circle there is no beginning and no end.
God's people are to walk hand in hand love we will send.
November 14, 2000

Love is a noun-naming or denoting action
Faith works by love
Knowledge without love is puffed up.

Impossible to please God without faith
There are many facets in love the first step is to accept
God's love. "*Jesus Loves Me.*"
Love causes faith to soar like an eagle.
When you get the spirit of faith you can:
(*Move That Mountain*)
If you have the spirit of Faith you will speak the words to:
(*Move That Mountain*)
I believe therefore I speak to the mountain.

Jesus—United We Stand (Song)

Chorus: United we stand in the presence of the Lord, giving honor
And glory to his name.
The kingdom of God is at hand:
The tomb is empty death is defeated in the land.
Washed in the blood of his love;
At one with *Jesus* was the message from above.
Life reigns; victory is the song.
Only the redeemed of *Jesus* can sing along.

Chorus:

April 4, 2002
"But seek ye first the Kingdom of God and his righteousness: and all
These things shall be added unto you" (Matthew 6:33).
"The Kingdom of God is not meat and drink, but righteousness and
Peace and joy in the Holy Ghost" (Romans 14:17).
Please read: Matthew 10:7; Matthew 16:19; Mark 1:15;
Luke 9:60; Luke 17:20–21; John 3:3

By Faith

By Faith Noah built an ark
By Faith the walls of Jericho fell down
By Faith Sara had a child
By faith Moses crossed the Red Sea on dry land.
They all died under the law of sin and death
Jesus destroyed this law; Now the Kingdom of God is at hand.
Jesus is the author of faith; he finished it on that old rugged cross.
We are now the heirs of the world; everlasting life is not a-far-off.
By faith through grace we are saved.
Hearing the word faith comes out of your mouth: your heart is
    bathed.
Hearing the word must be mixed with faith to profit you.
Faith and patience; the promises of God will come too.
There is no need in climbing the mountain, just speak to the moun-
    tain today.
Stand on the spoken word; impossible unbelief will say.
Getting your mind renewed in the word will cause the spirit of faith
    to soar.
Believe therefore speak the answer into existence; the spirit of unbe-
    lief will
Exit the door.
We are to fight this good fight of faith every day.
Be steadfast with thanksgiving all the way.

April 10, 2002
Please read: 2 Corinthians 4:13; 2 Corinthians 5:7

The Lord Is Worthy... (Song)

I...will praise the Lord...
I...will praise the Lord...
For he is worthy...
Oh yes he is worthy...
I...will serve the Lord...
I...will serve the Lord...
For he is worthy...
Oh yes he is worthy...
I...will love the Lord...
I...will love the Lord...
For he is worthy...
Oh yes he is worthy...
And... I will sing unto the Lord...
A new song...A new song...
Holy... Holy... Holy is the Lamb... Holy...

July 4, 2002

The Beautiful City (Song)

(Chorus) We're marching we're marching…
We're marching up to that city…
The beautiful City of Zion the Beautiful city of God…
We've be washed in the blood of the Lamb…we've put
On a robe of pure white…

(Chorus)

We are that city…
The beautiful city…chosen from above.

(Chorus)

We're putting on the Spirit man…
Walking in a newness of life.
Marching up to that city…
That beautiful city…
For the Crown of life…(Chorus)

August 11, 2002

Must Be Love (Song)

(Chorus) This must be love, friend…
This must be love, friend…
This must be love, friend…
The blessing of Abraham he's given to you. (Chorus)
He died upon Calvary; To set you free…

(Chorus)

Jesus said it's finished; Death no longer reigns…

(Chorus)

Jesus gave the keys to life forevermore; Now open up the door…

(Chorus)

The Good News tells the end; The Love of *Jesus* wins…

(Chorus)

April 23, 2003

In Jesus's Name

When you've cried and cried…and your heart is broken…
And you just want to hide.
You've prayed and prayed…hope can not
Be found…
Like a mighty rushing wind deep within.
Speak to the mountain
In *Jesus's* name.
When the seeds of doubt have clouded your mind…
And the peace
In *Jesus* can't be found.
Like a mighty rushing wind deep within.
By His Stripes you are
Healed in *Jesus's* name.
In *Jesus's* name every mountain falls in
The name of *Jesus*.

August 7, 2003
This was written after a year of pain and my spirit was broken.
Jesus healed my body.

Life Benefits

Washed cleansed by the blood of the Lamb; our sins were nailed
To the cross.
The curse of the law of sin and death is no longer the boss.
Redeemed from the curse of the law of sin and death;
Jesus closed the door.
All the benefits are yours; the key to life forevermore.
Death no longer reigns;
A new creation is the kind.
The spirit of love and a sound mind.
Your youth is restored like the eagle, made anew.
Bless the Lord O my soul is past due.
A promise of blessings for Abraham's seed comes into view.
Blessed wherever you go and blessed whatever you do.

October 27, 2003
Please read Psalms 103:5

Christmas

C is for Christ. *Jesus Christ* the anointed one, came to earth as
A baby boy.
H is for Hark. Hark the angels sang good news of great joy.
R is for Right. Right now we need to stop and think.
What does Christmas mean to me.
I is for Imagine. Imagine where and what would you be if it hadn't been
For *Jesus*, my mind can't conceive.
S is for Savior. A Savior who died and suffered on a cross for a world that
Lost in death and sin.
T is for Time.
Time to understand
Jesus defeated sin and death; we are
No longer under this law, the choice is there death or life
For women and men.
M is for Magnify.
Magnify *Jesus* and lift him up for he is Lord of Lords
And King of Kings praise his holy name.
A is for All. *Jesus* gave his all.
We are to love him the same.
S is for Speak.
Speak the word no guile, love, and forgiveness the
Kingdom flowing righteousness, peace, and joy.

November 3, 2003
Christmas means love, the beginning of the Kingdom of God Being
restored;
Jesus came as a baby boy.

Jesus Is Here (Song)

(Chorus) No matter what comes…
No matter what goes…
Jesus is here to see you through.
He hears every pray;
'Cause *Jesus* is here to see you through.
He sends forth his word and the power is here.
The wisdom is here to meet every need.

(Chorus)

Give him praise, the healing is here.
'Cause *Jesus* will wipe away the tears.
Give him praise he'll make a way.
He'll turn your darkness into day. (Chorus)
Jesus Is Here

February 14, 2004

Praising Jesus (Song)

You are the air of me.
You are the song that I sing.
You are my everything.
You are the Lord of Lords.
You are the King of Kings.
Your promises will always stand.
Your love has covered the land.
Glory and honor, I lift up to you. Praising *Jesus*, all day through.

July 14, 2004

Narrow Road to Life

This road of life is a narrow way.
This road is not found in darkness.
Jesus the light of day.
This road is located in a forest with many things to darken
The way.
If your mind is not renewed in the word daily, wrong words you
You will say.
There are stones in the road, you'll stumble and fall.
Get up praising *Jesus* before stinking thinking has gathered
To call.
People are depicted as trees blocking the path of light.
Your mind is clouded, death, and unbelief affects your sight.
Behind a bush a roaring lion is hidden waiting for you to
Let down.
The world has crept in, he's got you, never even made
A sound.
This road is not an easy road, but *Jesus* will give you the keys
To life's door.
Very few that fine, 'cause you must be taught and receive the word;
To stay on the road for life forevermore.

July 16, 2004
Please read: Matthew 7:13–14; Matthew 15:14; Luke 8:13;
1 Timothy 3:6
Jesus said the road is narrow and few there be that find it.
If you haven't found the right road my pray is that you do.

Promises

Many things you can't count on; the promises of God are
A sure thing.
The greatest promise was *Jesus*, even caused the angels to sing.
By the stripes of *Jesus* we were healed.
With the Holy Spirit of promise we were sealed.
The promise to Abraham was for the heirs of the world to be.
Through the righteousness of faith
Jesus gave light, now we can see.
The promises of the world are always a blunder.
In the Bible, the promises of God are a great number.
Hearing the word of God over and over, learning the wisdom
Of *Jesus* is the start.
You will speak these promises when they enter the heart.
Jesus speaks from his heart, spirit and life came.
Action with true faith words, you can do the same.

November 21, 2004
Read the following: Acts 2:33; Acts 13:23; Galatians 3:14–29;
Romans 4:13; Hebrews 10:22; 2 Peter 3:4–13;
Colossians 1:23; Ephesians 1:13; 1 John 2:25;
2 Timothy 1:1

The Mighty Angel

I know a man who walked the shores of Galilee.
He healed the blind, he healed the sick and set them free.
Now he's walking in the heart of man,
Leading and guiding into the promise land.
A mighty messenger clothed with spiritual words has come.
The mystery "God in You" will be for some.
This book of life is taught at the messenger's feet.
Renewing the mind, eating from the Father's table is the best seat.
God's promise is for a people that have washed their robes
In the Blood of the Lamb.
For they are blessed coming in going out and blameless before
The great *I Am*.

January 7, 2005
Revelation 10 (tells the story)

The Promises Living Way (Song)

I know a man who walked the shores of Galilee.
He healed the lame; he healed the sick and set them free.
Now he's walking in the heart of man.
Leading and guiding into the promise land.
Jesus has promised a new and living way.
The door is open this very day.
These wonderful promises God has for you.
Learn about the Holy Spirit of promise too.

January 7, 2004

Praises to Jesus Sing—(Song)

When I think about the wonder that you hold in your hand;
I think about your love that has covered the land.
(Chorus) Look toward heaven and this is what I say,
"You're every breath I take.
You're every song I sing.
Nothing no nothing can compare to the love, the joy that you bring."
When I think about how you died and rose from the grave.
I think about how you came to seek and to save.

(Chorus)

I think about your word that is renewing and healing for the soul.
I think about Calvary and how you washed my sins away;
The greatest story ever told.

(Chorus)

I think about the blessing, the treasure I hold.
I think about your
I Promises that will never go away.
I think about the victory you brought to life, and how the secret is in
The words that I say.

(Chorus)

December 19, 2005

The Way

There is only one way to *Jesus* it's called the way.
Jesus made the way when he died and arose that third day.
Judgement is there by the way or your own way.
Death will come to devour; the roaring lion will have his day.
Jesus said, "I am the way the truth and the life, come
Follow me."
When *Jesus* comes by find him;
Zacchaeus even climbed up
Into a Sycamore tree.
The way to *Jesus* is a straight and narrow road and very
Few that find it.
Seek and ye shall find; *Jesus* is the light of the world.
He's always lit.
The way to *Jesus* is found by seeking him with all your heart.
In the name of *Jesus* is the way; love, peace, and joy is only
A part.
The way is joy unspeakable and full of glory;
Healing, grace, prosperity, favor, and restoration just part of the story.
You choose the way is life forevermore today.
Jesus has sent a messenger to teach the way.

May 20, 2005
John 14:6; Matthew 3:3; Matthew 7:14; Nahum 1:3; Luke 19

Secret Things

Who can know the secret things of the *Lord Jesus Christ* today.

They are hid from the wise and prudent even if night and day they pray.

There is a new covenant revealed only to those that seek.

Seek and ye shall inherit the earth: it is for the meek.

All the treasures of wisdom and knowledge, there is a lid.

Only the righteous have the keys for others it is hid.

God reveals the deep and secret things to the righteous called out ones.

They dwell in a secret place under the protection of *Jesus* the son.

The righteous from the foundation *Jesus* knew.

Things kept secret from the foundation of the world shall be revealed to you.

June 1, 2005
Matthew 13:35; Psalms 91:1; Psalms 25:14; Romans 16:25;
Matthew 11:25; Matthew 5:14

Oppression

The Israelites were in oppression or bondage for 400 years.
Here comes Moses telling them of a promised land so wipe away
Your tears.
When you are oppressed, it's hard to be blessed.
Oppression keeps you from understanding with your heart.
Love and wisdom has left that's just a part.
Dwelling on the circumstances, a bad attitude increases
The mind is not sound.
This causes sickness to enter the body and more oppression
To keep you down.
To the death realm oppression is a giant key.
The truth is hard to see.
Joshua and Caleb made it to the promise land.
They kept focused on the truth and God's word.
Believing I will and I can.
Finding your way out of oppression is not an easy thing.
Jesus suffered oppression: we now have a new song to sing.
Focus on *Jesus* and what he has done.
Praising, giving thanks, and glory to *Jesus* the son.
Kingdom of God words is what we need to say.
All the promises of *Jesus* are for us today.

September 17, 2005
Oppression (definition) to weigh heavily on the mind, spirit, etc.
Burden to keep down. Physical and mental distress.
"Now therefore behold, the cry of the children of Israel is come
Unto me and I have also seen the oppression wherewith the Egyptians
Oppress them" (Exodus 3:9, KJV).

Isaiah 30:12; Isaiah 54:14; Ecclesiastes 7:7;
Keeping your mind and eyes on *Jesus* is the key.
Praising and giving Him praise for all he has done for you
Jesus Loves You

The Key of Life

Adam gave up the tree of life, to go with Eve.
The death realm reigned: so the Garden of Eden Adam
And Eve had to leave.
The law of sin and death even today reigns,
Until the truth of *Jesus* was revealed what he did
When he came.
His power has been freely given to you.
The chains of sin and death were broken too.
Jesus has locked the door to sin and death.
On the cross this took place with his last breath.
Jesus didn't say the truth and death, "I am the way."
He said, "I am the way the truth and the life.
I've come to give Life and more abundantly today."
There is no need to knock anymore.
You choose for the great I am became the door.
Jesus said, "I am the door.
I've given the key to life forevermore."

June 12, 2006 *Power* (definition) The ability to cause things to happen
John 10:7–9; Genesis 3:23–24; Romans 8:1–2; Romans 5:17;
1 Peter 2:24; Psalms 103

Jesus Is Here (Song)

(Chorus) *Jesus* is here
Jesus is here *Jesus* is here
To wipe away your tears
He has promised in his word.
Your prayers would be heard.

(Chorus)

Every little robin he promised he would feed.
Speak to the mountain he'll meet your every need.

(Chorus)

Because of his great love for you,
There's nothing he wouldn't do.

(Chorus)

November 12, 2006

Yes You Are (Song)

Yes you are yes you are
Yes you are the *Jesus* came as baby boy.
Yes you are the greatest love story.
Yes you are love, grace and glory.
Yes you are yes you are
Yes you are the glory in the darkest night.
Yes you are the morning star shining bright.
Yes you are the word giving light.
Yes you are yes you are
Yes you are the throne of grace your love has set me free.
Yes you are the lily, when all hope is gone you bloom for me.
Yes you are the glory of holiness for your people to see.
Yes you are yes you are
Yes you are grace and more grace; you are the open door.
Yes you are the Lords of Lords and King of Kings, so much more.
Yes you are everything no longer to be poor.
Yes you are yes you are
Yes you are my mercy when on the cross you died.
Yes you are my grace that's moving out the pride.
Yes you are my righteousness: came to live inside.
Yes you are life to me
Yes you are life to me

February 15, 2008

Glory, Honor, and Power Is Here

Turn back the pages of time and you'll see.
How man's glory, honor, and power ceased to be.
Adam and Eve disobedience caused sin and death to begin.
This disobedience now ruled man called sin.
God's love ruled so strong; he again wanted
Fellowship with men.
Only the Lamb of God could take away death and sin.
The ultimate price had to be paid.
All the sins of mankind on *Jesus* were laid.
To suffer and die, he then rose from the grave.
Jesus did this so man could be saved.
Man rose with him to life to those that believe.
Receiving this revelation your mind and spirit will
Not be deceived.
The Garden of Eden is now open.
Open again to those that believe.
Glory, honor, and power is here for those that will receive.
Continually praising *Jesus* every day,
Giving thanks and loving him is the only way.

November 12, 2006
Psalms 8:5; Psalms 138:5; Romans 2:7; Hebrews 13:15

The Kingdom Is Life

As I've wondered in this land.
I've seen how the devils had the upper hand.
But there's coming a day.
When God's people will have the say.
Jesus has made the way; he paid the price for
You and me.
You will find heaven for it will be.
A river of living water, righteousness, peace, and joy
Setting you free.
Power coming from God's people you see.
Sickness and death will no longer be a part of man;
Life will rule again.
The Kingdom of God will cover the land.

March 22, 2007
Ephesians 6:10; Acts 10:38; Proverbs 18:21; Psalms 145:11–13;
Romans 14:17;
"They shall speak of the glory of thy Kingdom and talk of thy power"
(Psalms145:11, KJV).

Jesus, You Are so Amazing

To my mom: Florence Pierce White

Jesus, you are so amazing, how you came to earth as a baby boy.
No one really knew what you came to do, not even the Angels.
When they sang for joy.
In the Old Testament Egypt is for an example, come into
The promise land.
The promise land today is why *Jesus* died for man.
Listen with your mind and your heart, take a seat.
Renewing the mind you must set at the teacher's feet.
Jesus, you are so amazing you won the victory; you fought
With love and death is what you killed.
With the Holy Spirit of promise until the day of redemption we
Are sealed.
Jesus, when you hung there on the cross forgiveness and
Love the whole world gained.
Jesus, you brought back life where death reigned.
Now your grace you took my place; you made me righteous.
The word is the light to see.
You came to restore, to set free, now sin no longer has a hold
On me.
Restoring the mind this is what brings the new mold.
Redeemed from the curse of the law: sin and death no longer
Has a hold.
Jesus, you are so amazing the glory of your holiness.
Praises and honor I lift only to you.
This Christmas remember the cross, the master of forgiveness.
Jesus changed the course of man too.

November 29, 2007
Romans 6:14 always remember
Jesus Loves You John 3:16

My Hero
To my Pastor—Rev. Richard G. Owings

Put this question before you: do you know of an earthly hero today?
Moses was in his day; he showed the children of Israel the way.
Jesus sent me an earthly hero. Richard Owings is my hero.
A teacher, evangelist, apostle, and pastor: most of all a prophet, the
World looks on and gives a zero.
When you search for truth *Jesus* will open the door.
I thank *Jesus* for giving me a teacher that teaches life and love
Forevermore.
Words can't express how much this message of life and grace
Means to me.
Jesus picked a hero and a prophet. I pray you have eyes to see.
In Revelations chapter 10, a prophet with a life message will
Take place.
A prophet will go around the world teaching life with lots and lots
Of grace.

October 12, 2008
Revelations 10 KJV

Your Time
To Audrey Atwood Pierce (my sister-in-law)

Roll back the pages of time and you'll see.
What *Jesus* has done for you and me.
He's conquered death and set the captives free.
The law of sin and death will no longer be.
Jesus made a way to the throne of grace.
So look to the cross and take your place.
We're no longer Pilgrims and strangers anymore.
The blessing of life: *Jesus* has opened the door.

January 4, 2009
Pilgrim (definition) a wanderer
Stranger (definition) an outsider, Visitor, newcomer
"For the law of the Spirit of Life in Christ Jesus hath made me free
From the law of sin and death" (Romans 8:2, KJV).

A New Song—Free

A new song I now can sing.
About the love *Jesus* brings.
Peace and joy that fills my soul.
The greatest story ever told.
When I look around and see.
All the good things you've done for me.
The cross, you paid the price: love grew into grace.
To set me free, you took my place.
The keys to life, you opened the door.
The blessing of life is grace forevermore.

April 19, 2009
Psalms 103

Coming a Day
To my brother—Robert Lee Pierce

As I've journeyed through this land,
I've seen how the devils had the upper hand.
But there's coming a day,
When God's people will have the say.
The chosen Sons of God a place they will find.
The words they speak will be with a renewed mind.
The Spirit of life; they will be filled.
The words of God will be their sword and shield.
God's glory will remain; For the power of God will reign.
Holy hands reaching out grace and mercy: only love Brings.
The beauty of his holiness will be seen.
Yes there's coming a day; God's people will have the say.
Holy, holy, holy to the Lamb;
Singing praises and honor to the Great I Am.

December 22, 2009
Ephesians 6:11–18, KJV

Jesus Is Already There

When this storm in your life has brought sorrow,
Jesus is there even in your tomorrow.
This mountain is higher and rougher than ever before.
Remember the battle is not yours anymore.
He's heard your prayers and your call.
Don't you know *Jesus* is in the center of it all.
His great big hand of grace is reaching for you.
The grace of *Jesus* is more than enough to get you through.
Jesus paid the price just for you.
Keep your eyes on *Jesus*; he has a miracle too.
Thanking *Jesus* is what you must do.
Loving and praising *Jesus* from your heart will get you through.

February 11, 2010
Jesus knows and cares about you; his love for you is so wonderful.
Romans 5:1–6, KJV

Love Is Jesus

We don't need another mountain.
We don't need another sky.
We just need to know you love us and
we're always in your eye.
We know your promises are true.
You'll always be there no matter what we do.
Your love is greater than anything I know.
'Cause you paid a debt we all owed.
You destroyed the law.
When you paid it all.
Your hands reached toward heaven; it's finished we go free.
These nailed-scarred hands now hold the key.
Now there is no need to knock for it's an open door.
Grace and blessings it's yours and mine, life forevermore.

May 20, 2010
JESUS LOVES YOU
Proverbs 10:22; 2 Corinthians 8:9

The Blood of Jesus

Many years ago, the blood of *Jesus* did flow.
The power in the blood all the world needs to know.
Jesus died to take your place; the greatest story ever told.
Nothing but the precious blood of *Jesus* can cleanse and make
You whole.
The blood became grace so the law could be erased.
The blood covers you with grace.
My friend now don't you worry for the blood is still at hand.
The blood of *Jesus* will set you free, only the blood can.
The blessing of *Jesus* can be. Then the Kingdom of God you can see.

January 14, 2012
Romans 5:8–17, KJV

The Prize

Keep your eyes on the prize
Keep your mind on the prize
The prize is *Jesus* the giver of life.
The blood of *Jesus* will cover you.
To restore and make you brand-new.
Narrow is the way and faith is the key.
A place the world cannot see.
The law keeps you bound; the good
News you can't see.
But the finished work of *Jesus* can set you free.

April 21, 2012
"For sin shall not have dominion over you: for ye are not under the
    law but
Under Grace" (Romans 6:14).

'Cause He Believed (Jesus)

Roll back the tables of time and you'll see.
How the devils had the upper hand and kept you in misery.
Through the promises of God, grace is here today.
When *Jesus* died grace made a way.
'Cause he believed in me.
'Cause he believed in you.
He paid the price.
To give you life.
When *Jesus* died there at Calvary.
He died to set you free.
'Cause he believed in me. 'Cause he believed in you.
When life has dealt you a bitter cup,
Remember the love of *Jesus* is more than enough.
Jesus said it's finished; the blood has covered thee.
No one but *Jesus* can set you free.
'Cause he believed in me. 'Cause he believed in you.

February 02, 2013
We are no longer under the law cause *Jesus* has set us free.
Free from the Law. Grace and more Grace is what JESUS has done
for you and me.
We have a new commandment "*To Love Another*"
Table: A compact. orderly arrangement of facts, figures, etc. usually
in rows and columns. The tables. laws, as the Ten Commandments,
inscribed on flat stone slabs.

Joy Comes in the Morning

I've been in the wilderness much too long.
All my hopes and dreams has lost the song.
I've took the test, I've done my best.
With all the stress and toil my body needs a rest.
But there seems to be no end.
All the hurt and tears are hard to mend.
When you look on my face, I hope you don't see.
The hopelessness that I feel that's really not me.
Jesus has given me grace to get me through the day.
So insanity can't find a way.
Jesus loves me and he died for me.
Things don't stay the same forever you see.
I'll keep holding on to *Jesus* come what may.
Joy comes in the morning;
I'm waiting for that day.

June 15, 2013
Let *Jesus* help you, no matter what has caused you pain in your heart.
Jesus is the great healer of a broken heart.

In the Presence of the Lord

In the presence of the Lord you'll see *Jesus*
In the presence of the Lord you'll see the King
In the presence of the Lord there is healing
In the presence of the Lord there is joy and peace.
In the presence of the Lord
There is nothing that you can't do.
In the presence of the Lord
When you say *Jesus* you've said it all.
In the presence of the Lord
Jesus restores and makes you anew.
In the presence of the Lord
There is love that covers you.
In the presence of the Lord
There is grace that sets you free.
In the presence of the Lord there is life forevermore.

August 01, 2013
Psalms 16:11 Please read

Do You Know Him? (Jesus)

For every breath that I take
For every song that I sing.
Praises I give to you
Though the storms of life may rage
but you always see me through.
Do you know him?
What he is…Love forevermore
Do you know him?
What he is…He's the Lily in the
Valley the Bright and Morning Star.
Do you know him?
What he is…Life Forevermore
Do you know him?
What he is…Wonderful *Jesus*
Do you know him?
What he is…Everything that's good…
Grace and Truth that's Forevermore.

June 12, 2014

Find the Road to Jesus (Grace)

The road that you're crossing, the chances of survival is very slim.
You're struggling viciously to get to the other side.
Knowingly it's a hot and vicious rim.
The other side has taken a toll.
It's even messed up your soul.
To get you back on the Jesus road,
Repentance is a seed that must be sowed.
The Jesus road is grace that made a way.
Grace is the key to life and renewing you today.
Jesus paid the price and grace sends a call.
Find the right road that leads to Jesus the healer of all.

June 14, 2014
This poem was written after watching a black woolly worm trying to
    cross a highway.
The day was hot and the road had intense heat.
The worm was trying so hard to reach the other side of the road.
This is what happens to people today.
They are looking for pleasure and something to please the flesh.
The wrong road many times is taken.
Jesus is the answer
"But seek ye first the kingdom of God, and his righteousness;
and all these things shall be added unto you" (Matthew 6:33).
"For by grace are ye saved through faith;
and that not of yourselves: it is the gift of God" (Ephesians 2:8).

In the Beauty/Praise

In the beauty of his holiness praise the Lord
In the beauty of his name *Jesus* praise the Lord
In the beauty of his promises...praise the Lord
In the beauty of his truth...praise the Lord
In the beauty of his power...praise the Lord
In the beauty of his
Love...praise the Lord
In the beauty of his *grace*...praise the Lord
In the beauty of his *forgiveness*...praise the Lord
In the beauty of his holiness...praise the Lord

August 11, 2014
Read: 1 Chronicles 29:13 and 2 Chronicles 20:21
We are to praise the Lord for all that he has done and loved us so
much.

Be Strong
(To my wonderful Teacher and Pastor: Rev. Richard G. Owings)

Be strong in the grace that Jesus gave
Walk in the grace
Sing in the grace love in the grace
Live in the grace
Jesus paid it all, giving you life.
He died in your place.
For the precious blood of *Jesus* that was shed became grace.
For the law keeps you bound.
Now grace you have found.
'Cause *Jesus* supplied the grace.
It's time to be strong in life and take your place.
He loved you so much love became grace.
Life forevermore; he died in your place.
Beautiful wonderful *grace* is the song.
Praising *Jesus* all day long.

September 26, 2014
"Thou, therefore, my son, be strong in the grace that is in Christ *Jesus*" (2 Timothy 2:1).

Blue Skies

I'm looking for blue skies
Where angels are singing, singing a new song.
Singing praises to *Jesus* all day long.
For this is the Kingdom of God;
Where peace, joy, and righteousness now waits.
This is the Garden of Eden, the angels guard the gate.
Grace has been freely given by *Jesus* you see.
The answer is love, *love* holds the key.

May 13, 2015
Please read Genesis 3:24

A Song—Amazing Grace
(To my son Brian Andrews and his wife Laura Andrews)

The day grace came to earth.
To give mankind a new birth.
This was the King of Kings born in a stable
To deliver was *Jesus*, the only one that was able.
Mercy and grace is reigning for all that will receive.
Jesus loved beyond the depths of sin. You now can believe.
Believe in the Savior that gave his all.
Grace in abundance has come to call.
Calling you into a realm where death and sickness no longer reigns.
Peace and joy you will also gain.
Jesus loved you so much he died in your place.
Giving you the song of *Amazing Grace*.

December 09, 2015
"Even when we were dead in sins, hath quickened us together with Christ by grace ye are saved" (Ephesians 2:5).
Please read: Romans 5:13–21
Jesus Loves You
James 4:6

Storms of Life
(To all that have lost a loved one)

When the storms of life is pouring;
And the hurt has left you with tears of mourning.
You now only have memories of yesterday;
A loved one has gone away.
A broken heart is hard to mend.
Even hard for a smile or grin to send;
Just up the road a little piece.
The sun is shining bright.
The flowers are blooming; you know the peace and grace that
Jesus gives you'll be all right.
The love of *Jesus* is an open door.
His amazing grace keeps on shining forevermore.

March 27, 2017
My husband passed away January 30, 2017 with dementia Alzheimer.
Sixteen (16) years struggle that was hard to bear watching him day by
day, week by week, month by month, and year by year.
"My grace is sufficient for thee" (2 Corinthians)
"Be strong in the grace that is in Christ *Jesus*" (2 Timothy 2:1).
"Grace and truth came by *Jesus Christ*" (John 1:17).
"Singing with grace in your hearts to the Lord" (Colossians 3:15–17).
"Grow in grace" (2 Peter 3:18)

Are You in the Lions' Den?

The lion den is where trials and battles take place.
This roaring lion is the devil seeking out he is on your case.
Daniel in the Bible was a wonderful example to follow for today.
He loved the Lord and the wisdom that was given him; guided him in
Whatever came that way.
Daniel loved and worshiped the Lord; this was his
Lions mouth closing key.
The devils' mission is to seek, destroy, and kill; that's the lion den
You see.
Daniel never had this amazing grace.
Grace that comes and sets you free from the law of sin and death;
And from the lion's place.
Keep your love and eyes on *Jesus* he'll get you through.
Jesus will close the mouth of the lion and you'll be stronger too.

August 20, 2017
Daniel 6, KJV

Worship the King

When you worship deep within your heart;
Joy and peace comes and healing can start.
Healing from a broken heart, grief, or stress, just knowing
Jesus has the answer for you.
Physical healing for the body will come too.
Remember amazing grace that was given, when
Jesus took your place.
All your sins he totally erased.
Thinking and thanking *Jesus*, and putting aside me.
Finding that praise realm will set your heart a dancing you see.
Lifting your heart to *Jesus* and loving him.
The great I *Am* will put you in another realm.
A place where love dwells and peace and joy is found.
Praises lifting up *Jesus* in a joyful sound;
Music and songs, giving Jesus the glory even with a shout.
Loving *Jesus* from the heart is what life is truly all about.

September 5, 2017

Wealthy in Love

Wealthy is a word defined by earthy man;
Having lots of money, possessions, and land.
A new commandment *Jesus* gave that was altogether new.
You love one another as I have loved you.
God is love; the universe was wonderfully created by him.
Wealthy in love was his total realm.
The Bible even starts in Genesis with Cain and Abel;
Love was absent and continued on so *Jesus* came as a baby boy
In a stable;
To bring back love to mankind.
The cross was his love sign.
Jesus loved us so much he died in our place.
Our past, present, and future sins he totally erased.
Jesus died in our place so we can go free.
Wealthy in love is what *Jesus* wanted us to be.
Love is our credentials; loving our sister and brother;
Jesus wanted us to be wealthy in loving one another.

May 23, 2018
John 13:34; 1 John 4

The Spirit of Faith

Praises and love to *Jesus* lift.
The Spirit of faith is one of the nine gifts.
The Spirit of faith is a *Jesus* trait.
Positive thinking brings positive words of faith.
Believing the spoken words
At times you wait.
The world was created by words; words can bring joy or sad.
Speaking out of your mouth from the abundance of the heart comes
Good or bad.
The Spirit of faith was present in Abraham's day.
He believed in the promises;
God's word had to say.
Believing the words and staying humble;
Holding on to the promise even when others stumble.
Words are powerful; speaking the wrong words you lose.
Words can deliver death or life you choose.
The Spirit of faith *Jesus* taught.
Jesus called Lazarus to come forth; this was a great example;
Jesus Brought.
Words can bring death or healing it's an open door.
Hearing the word causes faith to soar.
Wrong words brings darkness of the night.
The Spirit of faith brings light.
Love is the key; faith works by love.
Keeping eyes on *Jesus*, and focusing on things above.

September 6, 2018

1 Corinthians 12:8–10 (tells of the nine gifts of the Spirit); 1 Corinthians 2:5; Galatians 3:14; Galatians 5:22–24; Romans 8:1–6; Ephesians 4:23; Ephesians 6:16 (KJV)

Many times we go through hard times in our life.

Jesus is always there to see you through; he is in the midst of every storm.

God's word is powerful speak to that mountain.

The Bible says let the weak say I am strong.

The Lord is the strength of my life; these words will help you.

This earth was formed by words; God's word is powerful.

David in the Bible was not a giant; he spoke to the giant.

The giant went down with only a small stone.

David said he would kill the giant and he did.

We have giants in our life, not like David's giant.

Speak and tell *Jesus* what you need; he loves you and wants to help you.

Speak out what you believe not what you see.

Wisdom comes from God; ask and you will receive wisdom from God.

If you need prayer; just call me and we will pray together.

Have a blessed day!

About the Author

Valerie Ann Pierce Andrews was born to the parents of Glenn Pierce and Florence Pennell Pierce in Iredell County, North Carolina.

Reared by her mother, grandmother—Laura Isa Ellis Pennell, and grandfather—Robert Lee Pennell in Boomer, North Carolina.

She has two sons, Brian Keith Andrews and Barry Wayne Andrews; two grandchildren Jake Henry Andrews and Alanna Grace Andrews.

She attended Boomer Elementary School and graduated from Wilkes Central High School. She also took some courses from Wilkes Community College.

She works at Boomer Post Office and loves the people here.

She attends Jesus Life Worship Center and the pastor there is Rev. Richard G. Owings.

Her present address is still Boomer, North Carolina.

Her grandmother—Laura Ellis Pennell passed away August 6, 1966. Her husband—Verne Meredith Andrews passed away January 30, 2017, missing them both.

Printed in the USA
CPSIA information can be obtained
at www.ICGtesting.com
LVHW050339041223
765602LV00010B/380